CONTENTS

BIGFOOT TYPES

No one has ever managed to capture a Bigfoot. Yet many eyewitness reports and lots of physical evidence from countries all over the world have been collected. These suggest that a large unknown ape may exist, but it can take several different forms...

BIGFOOT – This creature takes its name from the huge footprints that it leaves behind. Bigfoot has been sighted mainly in North America, usually in mountainous forest regions. It is humanoid, but much larger and with longer arms, and is apelike in appearance.

What is claimed to be a female Bigfoot was filmed in Willow-Creek, California, in 1967. It is undecided whether or not the footage is genuine.

YETI – The Yeti lives in the Himalayan regions of southern Asia. Its colour varies from white to dark reddish-brown.

YEREN – Yeren is the Chinese name for Wildman. Thought to be a giant ape species hunted to extinction thousands of years ago, this creature may still exist in the mountains of China. Scientists think there are big and smaller versions.

KAKI BESAR – Kaki Besar is Malaysia's version of Bigfoot. Sightings have been reported of a giant hairy creature in the jungle.

GRAPHIC MYSTERIES
BIGFOOT

SUP T

AND OTHER STRANGE BEASTS

ender

BOOK HOUSE

Designed and produced by
David West  Children's Books
7 Princeton Court
55 FElsham Road
London SW15 1AZ

Editor: Charlotte Cattermole

First published in 2006 by **Book House,**
an imprint of **The Salariya Book Company Ltd**
25 Marlborough Place, Brighton BN1 1UB

Please visit the Salariya Book Company at:
www.salariya.com

HB ISBN 1 905087 65 9
PB ISBN 1 905087 66 7

Visit our website at **www.book-house.co.uk**
for free electronic versions of:
You Wouldn't Want to Be an Egyptian Mummy!
You Wouldn't Want to Be a Roman Gladiator!
Avoid joining Shackleton's Polar Expedition!

A catalogue record for this book is available from the British Library.

Printed on paper from sustainable forests

Manufactured in China.

Could Bigfoot be a hominid, and so be another extension of the human species? Drawings such as this one of an early hominid point to a resemblance between humans and Bigfoot.

ALMA – Sightings of this creature are similar to Bigfoot reports. However, the Alma is meant to look more like the type of human known as Neanderthal, than like apes. These beings are thought to live in the Caucasus Mountains in Asia, formerly a part of the Soviet Union.

This photograph is thought to be of a Florida Skunk Ape. It was sent to a Florida sheriff's office.

FLORIDA SKUNK APE – This Bigfoot is said to live in Florida. Its name comes from the awful smell that it gives off. It is believed to be two metres tall.

YOWIE – There are two different types of Yowie that have reportedly been seen in Australia. Sightings date back hundreds of years to when Native Australians told of such creatures living in the forests.

ORANG-PENDEK – Sumatra's wildman is a short ape that walks on two feet. It is similar to an orangutan, but walks upright all of the time, not just for a few steps.

THE WILD WORLD

From small tribes in central Asia to campers in the United States, stories about creatures like Bigfoot have come from all the continents on Earth.

BIGFOOT HAUNTS

Rumours and sightings of huge apelike creatures in the American northwest date to the arrival of early settlers to the region. However, the first detailed account of Bigfoot was in 1811, when an explorer discovered large footprints near the Rocky Mountains in Canada. The Native Americans, who greatly respect Bigfoot, told the explorer that the tracks belonged to Sasquatch. Since then, other reports have come from all over North America, from Canada in the far north, to California in the south.

There have been many Bigfoot sightings in the Rocky Mountains in Canada and on the west coast of North America.

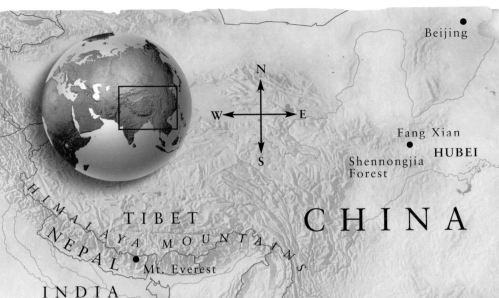

Beijing

N
W — E
S

Fang Xian
HUBEI
Shennongjia
Forest

CHINA

TIBET
HIMALAYA MOUNTAINS
NEPAL
Mt. Everest

INDIA

The dramatic scenery of China is home to many rare and unusual animals. Does it also hold the Yeren?

THE BAMBOO FOREST OF CHINA

The Hubei Province of central China is rich in legends and stories. It is still a relatively unknown and mysterious place. There are references from 2,000 years ago to the existence of strange apelike creatures, sometimes called Mountain Ogres. Ancient Chinese poets even wrote about such animals.

THE YETI'S ICY HOME

The name 'Yeti' is another term for 'abominable snowman'. This is because reports of the creature nearly all occur in the snowy regions of the Himalaya Mountains in Tibet. Yeti sightings have come from many sources, including experienced mountaineers and sherpas.

The white mountain slopes of the Himalayas may make it easier to spot a dark-furred Yeti. But they have also been seen in the thick forests that grow beneath the snowline.

INSIDE THE MONASTERY'S WALLS...

WELCOME. I AM THE MONASTERY'S ABBOT. WE DO NOT GET MANY VISITORS TO THIS REMOTE PLACE.

HI, MY NAME IS PETER BYRNE.

WHAT BRINGS YOU ALL THIS WAY?

I WORK FOR AN AMERICAN OIL COMPANY. WE WERE CHARTING THE AREA WHEN THE STORM BLEW IN.

WE KNEW YOUR MONASTERY WAS NEARBY, SO HERE WE ARE.

LET US GO INSIDE WHERE IT IS WARM.

WE WERE TOLD SOME STRANGE THINGS WHILE WE WERE DOWN IN THE VALLEY. TALES OF UNEXPLAINED MURDERS.

YES. NEWS OF THE CRIMES HAS REACHED US.

THE VILLAGERS ARE BLAMING SOME KIND OF MONSTER. THEY CALL IT THE YETI. THEY SEEM TO THINK YOU'RE AN EXPERT ON THE MATTER.

TELL ME WHAT YOU HAVE HEARD.

AT EACH VILLAGE THE STORY WAS THE SAME...

?!!!

THE VILLAGERS ARE
SUPERSTITIOUS.
THEY BELIEVE IN
THE YETI AND ARE
AFRAID OF IT.

SURELY YOU DON'T THINK THERE'S A MONSTER LOOSE IN THE MOUNTAINS? THE ATTACKS COULD HAVE BEEN MADE BY A BEAR, OR EVEN BANDITS.

THE MOUNTAINS HAVE SECRETS, MR. BYRNE. PEOPLE HAVE SEEN THINGS THAT ARE HARD TO EXPLAIN. LET ME TELL YOU COLONEL HOWARD-BURY'S STRANGE STORY...

IN 1921, COLONEL HOWARD-BURY LED A BRITISH EXPEDITION TO CLIMB MOUNT EVEREST.

THE CLIMBERS HAD BEEN MAKING GOOD PROGRESS.

SUDDENLY, HIGH ABOVE THEM ON A SNOWFIELD...

LOOK! UP THERE! SOMETHING'S MOVING!

WHO IS IT? THERE ARE NO OTHER CLIMBERS IN THE AREA!

THE CLIMBERS FINALLY REACHED THE SNOWFIELD.

WHAT ON EARTH...?!

THESE FOOTPRINTS... THEY'RE HUGE! WHO COULD HAVE MADE THEM?

NO HUMAN MADE THEM. IT WAS THE YETI!

SOME OTHER ANIMAL, A YAK PERHAPS, COULD HAVE BEEN WANDERING UP THERE. BY THE TIME THE CLIMBERS REACHED THE FOOTPRINTS, THE SUN MIGHT HAVE MELTED THE SNOW, MAKING THE PRINTS APPEAR LARGER.

FOOTPRINTS ARE NOT THE ONLY EVIDENCE WE HAVE...

ONLY LAST YEAR AN AMERICAN SCIENTIST, DR. NORMAN DYRENFURTH, MADE AN INTERESTING DISCOVERY...

HE WAS EXPLORING THE NEPALESE MOUNTAINS...

SHINE YOUR FLASHLIGHT OVER THERE. I THINK I SAW SOMETHING.

SCATTERED OVER THE CAVE FLOOR...

HUGE FOOTPRINTS! AND OVER HERE...

...IT LOOKS LIKE HALF-EATEN FOOD.

COULD THIS BE A YETI LAIR?

COULDN'T IT HAVE BEEN A SHELTER THAT THE LOCAL YAK HERDERS USED?

POSSIBLY. BUT LET ME TELL YOU CAPTAIN D'AUVERGNE'S STRANGE TALE. IT WAS 1938. THE CAPTAIN HAD GONE WALKING IN THE MOUNTAINS, ALONE...

...A BLIZZARD STRUCK AND...

...THE CAPTAIN BECAME LOST.

HE FELL, SNOW-BLIND AND EXHAUSTED.

HE AWOKE TO FIND HE WAS SAFELY OUT OF THE STORM. FOOD HAD BEEN LEFT FOR HIM.

THE CAPTAIN STAYED IN THE CAVE UNTIL HIS STRENGTH AND EYESIGHT RETURNED.

IF HE WAS SNOW-BLIND, HOW DID HE KNOW WHAT HAD SAVED HIM? NO, ABBOT, I'M STILL NOT CONVINCED THERE'S ANY SUCH THING AS A YETI.

15

COME WITH ME. I WISH TO SHOW YOU SOMETHING.

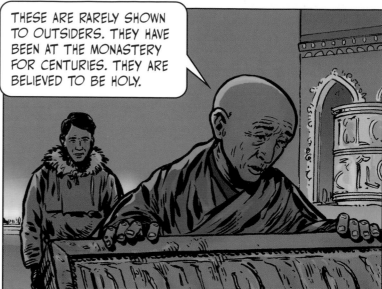

THESE ARE RARELY SHOWN TO OUTSIDERS. THEY HAVE BEEN AT THE MONASTERY FOR CENTURIES. THEY ARE BELIEVED TO BE HOLY.

THE RELICS! TOM SLICK WAS RIGHT, THEY ARE HERE!

THE SCALP AND THE HAND BONES OF A YETI.

MY EMPLOYER, MR. SLICK, IS A KEEN COLLECTOR OF UNUSUAL ITEMS LIKE THESE. HE WOULD...

HE'S A TEXAS MILLIONAIRE. HE'LL PAY WHATEVER YOU ASK.

MR. BYRNE, THE RELICS ARE NOT FOR SALE!

THE RELICS MUST NEVER LEAVE THIS MONASTERY.

BY MORNING THE STORM WILL HAVE DIED DOWN...

YOU AND YOUR SHERPAS CAN REST HERE UNTIL THEN. SLEEP WELL.

LATER...

I FEEL BAD ABOUT TRICKING THE OLD ABBOT LIKE THAT, PRETENDING I DIDN'T BELIEVE IN YETIS. BUT I NEEDED TO GAIN HIS TRUST SO HE'D SHOW ME WHERE THE RELICS ARE.

I KNEW HE'D NEVER SELL THEM, THOUGH. TOM SLICK ASKED ME TO GET HIM PROOF THAT THE YETI EXISTS...

...SO THAT'S WHAT HE'LL GET.

ALL I HAVE TO DO IS TO MAKE THE SWITCH AND...

WAKE UP! WE HAVE TO GO. NOW!

BOSS! THIS STORM...

I'M PAYING YOU TO WALK, NOT TALK. KEEP MOVING!

THOSE FINGER BONES I GOT IN KATHMANDU WERE WORTH EVERY PENNY.

THE MONKS WILL NEVER FIND OUT. AS FAR AS THEY KNOW, THEY'VE STILL GOT THEIR YETI BONES...

WELL, MOST OF THEM!

THE STOLEN YETI BONES WERE SNEAKED BACK TO LONDON. THERE THEY WERE SEEN BY DR. W.C. OSMAN-HILL. AT FIRST HE SAID THEY WERE HUMAN.

LATER, HE CHANGED HIS MIND, SAYING THEY WERE NOT HUMAN. SHORTLY AFTER, THE BONES DISAPPEARED – AND HAVE NOT BEEN SEEN SINCE.

THE END

THE WILDMAN OF CHINA

WHO IS HE? IS HE IMPORTANT?

YES. HE'S A SCIENCE PROFESSOR FROM BEIJING.

YOU KNOW HIM?

HE'S MY BOSS. AND I'M LATE FOR WORK! HERE, BUY SOME NEW VEGETABLES.

THANKS!

THE HEADQUARTERS OF THE SHENNONGJIA FOREST YEREN EXPEDITION...

AH! DOCTOR ZHOU, COME IN. I READ YOUR EXPEDITION REPORT. IT'S NOT BAD. IT'S A PITY YOU DIDN'T FIND A WILDMAN, THOUGH.

PROFESSOR.

I DON'T KNOW IF WE SHOULD CARRY ON WITH THIS RESEARCH, DOCTOR. IT COSTS MONEY, AND WITHOUT A WILDMAN TO SHOW FOR IT... WELL, IT'S HARD TO SEE WHY WE SHOULD CONTINUE.

WE DID FIND NEW EVIDENCE, PROFESSOR! FOOTPRINTS, DROPPINGS, AND LOOK...HAIR!

AND SOME OF THE EYEWITNESS REPORTS ARE GOOD TOO. THE FIREWOOD GATHERERS FROM SHENNONGJIA - THEIR STORY IS VERY STRONG.

THE FIREWOOD COLLECTORS? YOU'LL HAVE TO REMIND ME...

19

THOCKKK!

LIAO CONGGUI AND HIS NEPHEW WERE GATHERING FIREWOOD IN THE SHENNONGJIA FOREST.

THIS FOG'S GETTING THICKER. NEPHEW, KEEP CALLING OUT SO I KNOW WHERE YOU ARE.

I CAN HARDLY SEE A THING NOW...

WHERE ARE YOU? SHOUT OUT!

GRUNT!

STOP PLAYING GAMES, LAD! I DON'T SCARE **THAT** EASILY!

GRUNT! GRUNT!

GRUNT!

SNAPPP!

HUH?!

WHO'S THERE?

YES. A BELIEVABLE STORY, BUT...

I HAVE SUPERIORS TOO, DOCTOR. THEY ONLY WANT TO KNOW WHEN THEY CAN SEE A YEREN IN A CAGE.

IF THEY STOP THE RESEARCH, THAT MAY NEVER HAPPEN.

AND WE DID COME SO CLOSE TO SUCCESS...

THE 1977 EXPEDITION TO THE SHENNONGJIA FOREST HAD BEEN ONE OF THE LARGEST OF ITS KIND. IT WAS DUE TO LAST ALMOST ONE YEAR. AS WELL AS SEARCHING FOR THE YEREN, THE SCIENTISTS ALSO STUDIED THE FOREST'S PLANT AND ANIMAL LIFE.

WITH THE SCIENTISTS WERE HUNTERS WITH TRANQUILISER DARTS, SCOUTS, AND SOLDIERS. IN ALL, MORE THAN 100 PEOPLE WERE INVOLVED. DOCTOR ZHOU WAS THE HEAD OF A SPECIALISED GROUP THAT TRAVELLED DEEP INTO THE HEART OF THE MOUNTAINS.

CAN YOU SEE IT? IS IT MOVING, DOCTOR ZHOU?

IT'S JUST SITTING THERE. I DON'T THINK IT'S A BEAR.

MAYBE THE EXPEDITION WAS TOO BIG. DOZENS OF PEOPLE CRASHING THROUGH THE UNDERGROWTH WOULD HAVE SCARED EVERYTHING AWAY.

DO YOU BELIEVE YEREN EXIST, DOCTOR?

SOMETHING BIG IS OUT THERE.

HERE, LET ME READ YOU AN ACCOUNT OF THE FANG XIAN INCIDENT, PROFESSOR...

MAY 14, 1976. NEAR FANG XIAN, HUBEI PROVINCE...

A GROUP OF GOVERNMENT OFFICIALS WERE RETURNING HOME AFTER ATTENDING A MEETING.

SUDDENLY...

SLOW DOWN! LOOK!

HEY! WAKE UP!

SMART MOVE! NOW WE'LL NEVER KNOW WHAT IT WAS!

THE STORY SOUNDS BELIEVABLE. WHY WOULD GOVERNMENT OFFICIALS LIE?

PERHAPS WE SHOULD LEARN FROM THE EXAMPLE OF THE WOODCUTTER AND HIS NEPHEW. STAY IN ONE SPOT AND LET THE YEREN COME TO US.

HMM. I THINK YOU CAN CARRY ON WITH YOUR RESEARCH AFTER ALL, DOCTOR.

I SHALL TELL MY SUPERIORS THAT WE HAVE TO FIND OUR WILDMAN...

BEFORE THE AMERICANS CATCH THEIR BIGFOOT!

NEARLY HOME NOW.

HI, GRANDMA!

AH, SANCHING, JUST IN TIME TO HELP ME SHELL THESE PEAS!

LATER, GRANDMA, I HAVE TO SEE GRANDAD FIRST. WHERE IS HE?

HE'S INSIDE.

GRANDAD! I HAVE THE FOOD.

GOOD BOY!

BIGFOOT

THE CABIN WAS NOT ONLY HOME TO THE MINERS...

RATS! I HATE THEM!

HOLD A LIGHT OVER THAT SACK OF POTATOES, FRED.

BLAMMM!

SQUEEEKKK!

PETE, IT'S A GOOD THING YOU CAN SHOOT STRAIGHT. BECAUSE...

THIS ISN'T A POTATO...

?!!

THERE'S ENOUGH DYNAMITE IN THIS POTATO SACK TO BLOW US ALL CLEAN OFF THE MOUNTAINSIDE!

OVER THE NEXT FEW DAYS, THE MINERS STARTED WORKING THEIR CLAIM, USING THEIR MUSCLES...

...AND THEIR DYNAMITE TO FIND THE GOLD SEAM.

BOOOMMM!

BUT IT WAS NOT LONG BEFORE THE MEN REALISED THAT SOMETHING WAS WRONG.

SCREEECHHH!

DID YOU HEAR THAT, FRANK?

I HEARD IT YESTERDAY, TOO.

WHAT IS IT?

I DON'T KNOW. IT DOESN'T SOUND LIKE ANY ANIMAL THAT I'VE EVER HEARD BEFORE.

THE STRANGE SOUNDS CONTINUED. THE MEN MADE SURE THEY WERE ALWAYS ARMED.

I'M GOING DOWN TO THE STREAM TO FETCH SOME WATER, FRED. WANT TO COME?

WELL, SURE FRANK.

BRING YOUR RIFLE.

33

SUDDENLY...

THERE'S SOMETHING BEHIND THOSE TREES!

BLAMMM! BLAMMM! BLAMMM!

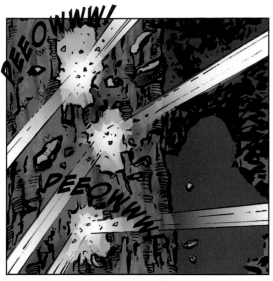

PEEOWWW!

PEEOWWW!

FRED SHOT AT THE CREATURE, TOO.

BACK AT THE CABIN...

WHAT'S ALL THE SHOOTING FOR, BOYS?

THERE'S SOME KIND OF CREATURE LOOSE IN THE WOODS!

FRANK AND FRED TOLD THE OTHERS THEIR STORY.

MAYBE IT WAS A LARGE BEAR, OR MAYBE AN ANIMAL THAT'S ESCAPED FROM A ZOO OR CIRCUS?

WHATEVER IT WAS, IT'S TOO LATE TO DO ANYTHING NOW. IT'LL SOON BE DARK.

THEY DECIDED TO TURN IN FOR THE NIGHT. THEY PLANNED TO PACK UP AND LEAVE AT SUNRISE...

ZZZZZ

MIDNIGHT...

BANG!

UH?

KERRRBANG!

BANG!

CLANNNG!

GET UP! SOMEONE'S THROWING ROCKS AT THE CABIN!

36

THE MEN LOADED THEIR CAR.

WHAT ABOUT ALL OUR MINING GEAR? IT'S WORTH A LOT OF MONEY.

STAY AND GUARD IT IF YOU LIKE, JOE.

LOOK!

OVER THERE!

ROARRRR!

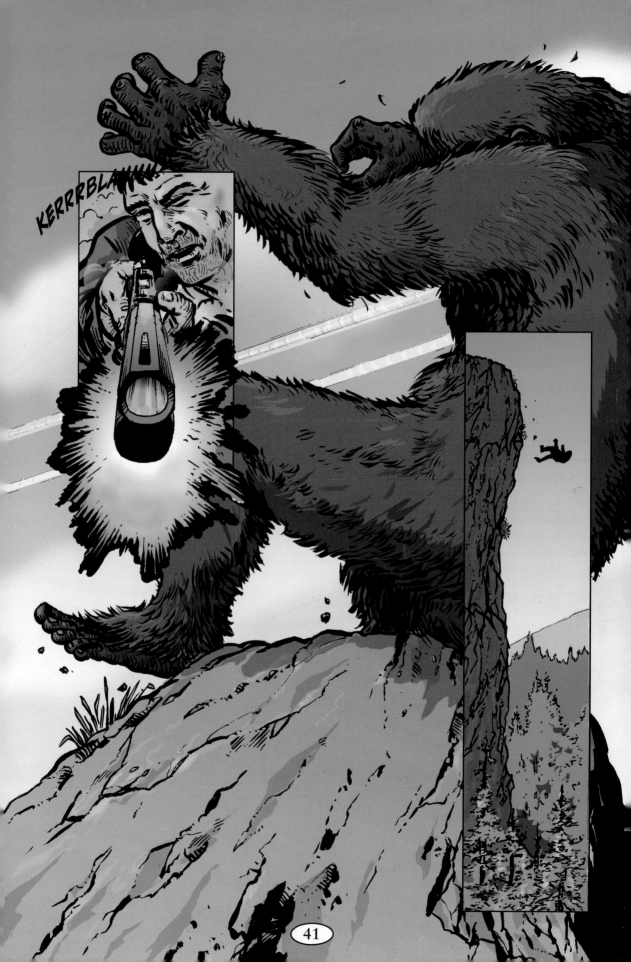

KERRRBLA

THE FOUR MINERS LEFT AS QUICKLY AS THEY COULD...

BACK IN THE NEARBY TOWN OF KELSO, THE MINERS' STORY SPREADS...

READ ALL ABOUT IT! APEMEN ATTACK MINERS!

APEMAN ATTACK!

FRED, I'M TELLING YOU. THIS WHOLE TOWN'S GONE APEMAN CRAZY!

PEOPLE FROM ALL OVER THE COUNTRY ARE TURNING UP HERE, WANTING TO SHOOT ONE OF THESE MOUNTAIN DEVILS. SEE THAT GUY OVER THERE? HE'S COME ALL THE WAY FROM ENGLAND! HE OWNS THE BIGGEST RIFLE I'VE EVER SEEN. HE MUST THINK WE'VE GOT ELEPHANTS ROAMING THE WOODS!

THE PLACE IS CRAWLING WITH NEWSPAPERMEN, TOO. A REPORTER FROM PORTLAND WANTS ME TO SHOW HIM THE CABIN AND MAYBE FIND THE DEAD APEMAN...

FRED AND THE REPORTER REACHED THE BOTTOM OF THE CLIFF...

...AND THAT'S AS FAR AS I'VE GOT. NOW, WHERE'S THIS DEAD APE?

IT SHOULD HAVE LANDED AROUND HERE SOMEWHERE.

42

THE END

FACT OR FICTION?

Are these accounts of large, hairy creatures actually sightings of Bigfoot? Do the many tracks and footprints found come from Bigfoot beasts or just wild animals?

Casts of footprints like these have helped to make Bigfoot world news.

IS THERE ANYTHING OUT THERE?
Taken together, the thousands of sightings of Bigfoot creatures indicate that this is a matter that requires careful study. They have encouraged scientists to look more closely at these cases.

FOOTPRINTS IN THE SNOW
It is possible that tracks in the snow, such as those found by the explorer Eric Shipton in 1951, were made by the local people of the Himalayas, who can walk on snow without shoes.

Could there be large animals hidden away, still waiting to be found? The African mountain gorilla was not seen by Western explorers until 1902.

CAUGHT ON CAMERA

Filmed sightings of Bigfoot creatures are rare. Roger Patterson's Willow-Creek footage, shot in California (see page 4), is the best to date. It has divided people into those who believe it is real and those who think it is someone dressed in a costume.

A SCIENTIFIC APPROACH

Many scientists are doubtful about the existence of Bigfoot, as there is not enough solid evidence. But with the discovery in recent years of many new and large animals, they are starting to accept that Bigfoot might be another creature waiting to be found.

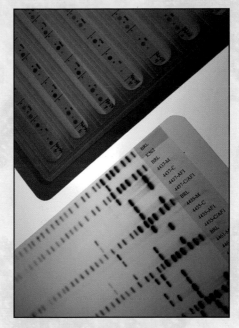

Scientists are now testing the DNA in hair samples to see whether they could belong to Bigfoot. The genetic tests will see if they match up to human or ape hair, or to the hair of any other species.

HOAXES

Some people have admitted, after several years of keeping their secret, that they lied about their sightings and made up evidence. Ray L. Wallace said that he had created the famous Bigfoot tracks found in California in 1958.

The possible existence of apemen has fascinated us for centuries. This picture was drawn in the sixteenth century.

GLOSSARY

abbot The senior monk in a monastery.

claim Something that one declares ownership over, such as a plot of land.

embankment The raised edge of something, mainly a river, road, or railway.

extinction No longer existing.

genuine The real thing.

Himalaya Mountains The world's highest mountain range. It is in Asia and covers Nepal, Tibet, India, Pakistan, and Bhutan.

holy When something is spiritually pure, godly, or sacred.

hominid Member of the species that humans belong to.

humanoid Something that has the same basic appearance as a human being.

incident A specific event.

Kathmandu The capital city of Nepal.

lair The home of a wild animal.

monastery A place that is home to a community of religious people who eat, live, and pray together.

monk A male member of a religious community.

mortar A mixture of cement, sand, and water that is used in buildings to join bricks.

Neanderthals One of the earliest forms of human on Earth.

Nepalese Mountains Part of the Himalaya range, it has 14 of the world's highest mountains.

prospector Someone who explores an area, usually for minerals.

relics An object that has been preserved and is highly thought of.

remote Somewhere that is far away from anything else.

research An investigation or examination of something, and the information uncovered by such an investigation.

Sasquatch Native American name for Bigfoot.

semester One of two terms in the academic year.

Sherpa An expert guide of the Himalaya Mountains.

snow-blind When sunlight reflects off the snow causing pain and sensitivity to light in the eyes.

superstitious To be influenced by a fear of the unknown or the supernatural.

tranquiliser A drug used to calm something or send it to sleep.

undergrowth Shrubs and bushes that grow in a forest.

yak A long-haired ox from Tibet.

FOR MORE INFORMATION

ORGANISATIONS

Bigfoot Discovery Museum
5497 Highway 9
Felton, CA 95018
www.bigfootdiscoveryproject.com

Bigfoot Field Researchers Organisation
www.bfro.net

FOR FURTHER READING
If you liked this book, you might also want to try:

The Loch Ness Monster and Other Lake Mysteries
by Gary Jeffrey, Book House 2006

Bigfoot: Man, Monster, or Myth?
by Carrie Carmichael, Steck-Vaughn 1997

Bigfoot: Opposing Viewpoints
by Norma Gaffron, Greenhaven Press 1988

Guide to the Unexplained
by J. Levy, DK 2002

In the Footsteps of the Russian Snowmen
by Dmitri Bayanov, Pyramid Publications 1996

INDEX

Web Sites

Due to the changing nature of Internet links, the Salariya Book Company has developed an online list of Web sites related to the subject of this book. This site is updated regularly. Please use this link to access the list:

http://www.book-house.co.uk/grmy/bigfoot